WITHIN
WITHOUT

First Edition: 2021

ISBN: 978-81-947103-5-6

Book Design: Vivechana (www.soulscapes.in)
Images: www.unsplash.com
Image Editing and Recolor: Vivechana

Published by
Soulscapes
Mumbai, India
Website: www.soulscapes.in
Email: info@soulscapes.in

Printed in India

WITHIN WITHOUT

a collection of reflective poetry

Upasana

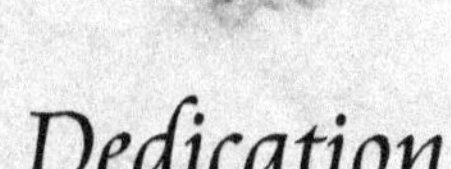

Dedication

To Leela Saraf
who gave me life

To Meeta
who taught me how to live

Contents

Foreword

Upasana Saraf is an ardent believer of love and beauty and considers herself as an extremely private person. Yet as a poet, she has a lot to convey and explore in both her real and imaginary worlds. Her poems are visceral, hard-hitting and arises directly from her intense experiences, especially emotional ones that often leave her distraught and puzzled; only because she is so passionately invested in them. Her poems are refreshing to read as there's no sugar-coating hidden in clever metaphors when she's writing about what she perceives and feels.

> In her poem 'Choices' she says,
> *It is as it was*
> *meant to be*
> *You are this you*
> *and I am this me*
>
> *There is no turning back*
> *all regrets are in vain*
> *If we returned to where we were,*
> *We would still be here yet again.*

In all the torment and leave-takings that her poems are replete with, there's an innate wisdom – the wisdom of not holding on, or for that matter, holding back. When Upasana reads and observes people and situations around her, she doesn't exclude herself.

> *I had been so many versions*
> *I was losing track*
> *I only knew that someday I had*
> *to find myself back*
>
> *I still lost you anyway*
> *and oh! The irony*

'twas cause I ceased to be
the person that was me. – 'Expectations'

The poems in *Within Without* draw you in again and again as something tells you that here's a poet who speaks her truth, and not just her truth but yours as well. She then exposes those corners of your heart and mind which you guarded so ferociously all your life. And that is the universality of her thought processes that readers identify with.

In 'The House of Cards', she writes,
Cracks had widened beyond repair
Cards were scattered everywhere
Maybe the missing ones had weakened it
or the broken ones that did not fit

Through her poems, Upasana displays tremendous fortitude showing you how life can be dealt with by looking at it square for all that it offers, and that there's no need or scope for escape. And when one does that, it's possible to have the love, all of nature's beauty and innocence restored, returned to us – intact.

In some startling lines, Upasana writes,
The thoughts that rise in me
My pen that wills to write
Mere words to forget
Coloured dreams of the blind. – 'Conflict'

and, in 'Solitude':
I need space around me
And time to shift things about
I need no distrustful emotions to be
I can be within without.

Gayatri Majumdar,
Writer, Publisher and Editor
Founder of The Brown Critique literary journal

Introduction

This book is replete
with insane words
of an arrogant ego.
The dissatisfactions
and complaints
of an immature mind
whom
restless emotion
renders totally blind.

Read if you must
and eke of it
what you can
Maybe you'll find
a part of you
in these words filed
Or read if
only to indulge
a self-centred child.

The feelings were real
The hope and laughter too
Passion and impulse
Impatience and wisdom
Throwing life askew
The words meant a lot
Helped me ease the pain
For what Time takes away
Memory brings again.

You may never understand
what is written
in its personal spirit
For what is special
to the poet
is just style and rhyme
to the reader –
The borders invisible
of her space and time.

Poetry is a private world
that lies open to all
Walk in and out
as strangers
For it is a home
for gypsy thoughts
If you recognize one
stay and talk
or leave, if not.

Flowers of May – I

So far, today,
From the beauty I loved so
The leaves of Autumn
The flowers of May
The path had beckoned
And I, sure of being with it,
Halted on the way
It was my choice, I reckoned
Never thinking
When one lane met another
And I walked
Further and further away
Till all the singing
Had died away unnoticed
I was going to
Turn back one day
Return to my Autumn leaves
And my flowers of May
But as one way
Led on to another
I'd left them so far behind
They seemed unreachable

I look upon them now
as one would a memory
of a faded photograph.
In all that I had gained
So much had been lost
Who can say
What might have been,
Time holds its secrets
Never to reveal
If I could
Just go back one more time
To the grassy days
When tall trees beckoned
And leaves turned red in Autumn
And the flowers spread out
In the meadows of May
I would never come back, I reckon.

Sacrosanct

I have had to learn once more
How I should never open the door
to strangers, as my mother once taught me
when I was a child and filled with curiosity.

"If you did", she would say,
"they perchance might take away
What you hold most precious to you
So be cautious who you open the door to".

Wisely I heeded my mother's advice
And always checked the other side
Till I forgot the words one day
And thought true love had come my way.

He was a stranger and fascinating
I unlatched the door and let him in
"Fear not, mother, for I am now mature,
What if it's opportunity knocking at my door?

"He might become my friend for life
Or maybe one day make me his wife.
Unless he comes in how will I know,
Whether he is friend or foe?"

"You may be older but to me
You'll always be a child of three
I told you once, love, be cautious,
You must know and choose your guest".

"Oh mother darling, I regret
That your wise words I did forget

He took away my heart with him
The guest who I let carelessly in.

"Now I keep the door firmly shut
And open it to no one – but
They all look like strangers to me
Inside my house, I'm lonely".

My mother smiled and held me close
"Open your door to only those,
Who on finding the door shut
Do not force it open, but

Come again some other day
And ask politely if they may
Help you to open the door
With patience, caring, and lots of love".

Again a knock and I was scared
Not knowing who I might find there.
Pressing my back to the door
Hoping for something to reassure.

"Welcome", he said, "into my world,
For inside you have too long suffered
There is sunlight, hope, and lots of care
It is my home that we can share".

I stepped outside in wonder and surprise
And stayed to enjoy his world outside.
And one day the courage I did find
To lead him in through the doors of my mind.

My own true love is now here to stay
I thank you, mother, for your words that day.

The Day We Met

My life began the day we met
Before that, I know not yet.

The sun had risen in its usual place
The day began at its routine pace
Chores to be done, schedules set,
On the morning of the day we met.

I got dressed with usual impatience
To set out for the halls of education
Wondering if I'd left the gas on again yet
Thus began the day we met.

I trudged on wearily for another day
Waiting for time to pass away
Classes to know, learning to forget,
A usual day on which we met.

I dreamed, staring outside the window,
What was – I did not care to know
Oblivious except for wanting an outlet
Yes. A routine day on which we met.

I did not see or mark an identity
Of the person who sat right next to me
I felt nothing – just disinterest
The first moment of when we met.

Then you smiled and asked my name
I replied, then did the same.
Formal strangers, our lives a secret,
So we were, that day we met.

You were so eager, so ready to be friends
Such amicability I could not comprehend
To stretch my hand, I did hesitate
I was unsure, that day we met.

You were too nice to be true
I grant I was suspicious of you
A relationship I did not wish to regret
And so moved away, the day we met.

Now I bow in reverence to that day
And am glad I could not turn away
Friend, who I love and respect
With whom my sun rises and sets
My life began the day we met
Before that? I know not yet.

One Step at a Time

You listen seriously
as I speak
your eyes watching
as they seek
whether I meant
all that I said
or were they just words
that came to my head

What I said
Arose from my heart
it was honest
from the start
I knew you cared
it propelled me on
I had to give you time
It could take long.

I wanted you to know
The way I saw me
and in spite of masks
I wore for society
I took them off
for you to see
The person that I was
in my reality.

It was a risk
the path unknown
I travelled with you
Through grass and stone
I reached for your hand
you held it back
I walked on
Unsure of the track

It could not be trust
nor a lack of care
You had reasons I knew
that you did not share
I knew I walked
too fast for you
(you would smile at this,
as I did too).

There were many thoughts
in your mind
and I, walking on,
didn't look behind.
If you were with me
on this journey
I knew it meant
you could trust me.

Only when
the time is right,
will you walk
by my side
Till then we shall search
where the trail ends
and if, at the last,
we shall still be friends!

Magic

You filled my life with magic
You brought alive
Fairy tales I had read
In childhood
You showed me a world
I had long believed dead,
A world of knights
And love and loyalty,
Of rescuing lives
And happily ever-afters.
You gave me a life
Full of unbroken promises
Of deepest love
And intense friendship
You gifted me
The joy of open feelings
Unashamed emotions
Of truth
Of reality
You gave the world to me.

Love's Song

I love my love in all seasons
My love knows no rhyme, no reason.
My love has a trust that's blind
My love has a heart compassionate and kind.
My love has features like no other
My love is delicate like a flower
I respect my love more than me
I worship my love, and in my love believe,
My love that's reflected in my eyes
Is far more boundless than the skies
My love is sweeter than the sweetest potions
My love is profound as the deepest oceans
My love is wild and unrestrained
My love defies for earth what gods ordained
My love is unconditional and pure
My love is a malady that wants no cure
My love is tranquil as grassy paths in lonely forests
As secure as an old forgotten love-bird's nest
My love is calming like a quiet stream
My love is as wonderful as a precious dream
My love, like the sun, makes my day begin
My love rocks me to sleep when the night comes in
My love is a gem, both rich and rare
My love is tender feeling, faith and care.
My love for my love will always be
A love that lasts through eternity.

Infinity

Have you ever tried to
hold a sunbeam in your hand?
Or tried to catch a rainbow,
or clasp a fistful of sand?

Have you ever wished to
string moonbeams with stars?
Or to reach out and touch the sky,
or revive a withered flower?

If you had then you would know
the wonder of their existence,
And perhaps regret your audacity
to conceive such impertinence.

Thus so do I feel
when you ask me to write for you
To limit you within boundaries
of words, and adequately too?

Words may be stringed together
and yet none maybe justified.
For what can be put in words
is still finite.

A Moment in Time

A hundred years hence
It will make no difference
What we did and what we were
If we smiled or shed a tear
It won't matter if we loved,
Or if we got what we deserved
Nor what we wished and what we dreamed
If our life was as it seemed
Whether we knew or just believed
Living in ignorance of being deceived
They won't care for our integrity
Our loyalties, our honesty,
What we value, they may discard
And discredit what we reward.

And yet they will gaze at the sea,
Like we do today, you and me,
Revel in the splendour of the sky
Into the blue when the birds fly
They will sit on mossy stones
And sing songs of time long gone
Smile at flowers and the hum of bees
The fresh green grass 'neath the alder trees
And beside the merry, bubbling stream,
They will talk of wishes and dreams
And maybe the rainbow of the first rain
Will bring lovers together once again.
And the wheel of life will roll once more
While another century will close its door.

I Don't Miss You

No, I don't miss you

Except when the wind blows
Except when the flower grows
Except when the river flows
Except when the lantern glows
Only when the sky is blue
Only then do I miss you.

Oh yes, I think of you whenever
Stars wink shyly at each other
When sky and earth are seen together
When people talk of 'forever',
Whenever you are not with me, it's true,
I find myself thinking of you.

Can I miss you when you are in me?
The melody in my ear, the beauty that I see.
You're my music, art and poetry
You are in every kindness and generosity.
When anything is pure and true
I know it is but a part of you.

Often, I wish you by me I own
No one else but you alone
When the wind outside begins to moan
When the rose by it is blown
When memory makes its presence known
When shadows creep and pick at bones.

Do I then or don't I miss you
I cannot comprehend
So with these few lines
Maybe you will know, my friend.

Wishful

They say, thoughts
have immense power.
If I wish for you today,
Will you come?

They say, the voice
of sincerity must be heeded.
If I call your name,
Will you turn?

They say, memory
can recreate the past.
If I miss you today,
Will you think of me?

They say, dreams
can make anything happen.
If I dream of you,
Will you be reality?

I know you don't hear me
And if I had to guess,
In the fancy of my heart
The answer is always 'yes'.

For Adhira

Shining eyes and dancing feet
You cannot sit still in your seat
You always have so much to say
Captivated by your imaginary play

Your innocence shines through your guileless face
Your giggles and laughter invade every place
You fill my life with love and light
You are the most beautiful star of the night

You are the sunshine inside of me
A warm hug holding me eternally
Whether I am with you or apart,
I will always carry you in my heart.

Conflict

I find that I cannot
Share you with someone else
Yet that I cannot be enough
Clearly my experience tells.

I have never been one
To be part of a crowd
Partly because I'm scared
Partly because I'm too proud.

I need to be extreme
So I can stand apart from them
So if you cannot walk the mile,
I'll understand.

You tend to care for people
Something I love about you
And yet this very trait
Will separate us two.

That I can be unfair
Was something you knew
But that I am also fickle
Is known to very few.

Today you are dearer far than anyone
Tomorrow I do not know
And if you do walk away,
You would have wisely chose.

Respect you I always will
And work with you in the same old way
Yet some feelings will surface
And trouble you day by day.

Difficult I am, and will always be
But your strength will see you through
I trust you to do what is right
Right for me, and right for you.

The thoughts that rise in me
My pen that wills to write
Mere words to forget
Coloured dreams of the blind.

The Wall

You hide yourself
So well from all
It would seem
An impenetrable wall.

Sitting alone inside
You watch me and smile
Silent, unspeaking,
As is your style

I cannot hold
Your gaze for long
The impact is
Much too strong

I search in my mind
To say something right
Something you want to hear
For which you wait every night

Even if I knew it
I don't know the cost
If I wasn't right,
There'd be too much lost

I don't want to tell you
What you mean to me
In your trust and care,
There is deep vulnerability

You finish your coffee
And I finish mine
Feeling desperate within
Unable to prolong time

You are in no hurry
But I know it's time to go
The words don't come
And desert me once more

There will be other days
Other times we meet
Will it get easier
Or will silence repeat?

Nothing on your face
Shows me what you feel
What emotions lay there
So studiously concealed?

I think when alone
Of times we shared
When your look or gesture
Showed me you cared

The time you stayed back
The time you gave me your shoes
The time you quietly listened
In the early morning hues.

Times you travelled with me
Times you exchanged a look
Times you let me give you
My favourite music and books.

The time you lay asleep
Holding on to my hand
As the other stroked your hair
And caressed back a strand

The times your fingers searched
for mine
And finding them, reposed,
Smiled as I held you
To guard you against the cold

Still I wonder at the
Silent question in your eyes
And how long you'd wait
Till I got it right

Your thoughts still hide
Behind the wall unbroken
The words still silent
That are not yet spoken.

Scribbles

How can I ever tell you
How much you mean to me
Filling endless pages
With useless poetry.

My feelings cannot be
Contained within my heart
And I shall probably write
All the time we're apart.

I know you shall wonder
At this and raise your hand
In the old familiar gesture
To say you don't understand.

You'd tell me to stop
For this is crazy to you
I smile as I think of this
For I think it's crazy too.

And yet I must have you know
That this urge I cannot kill
When I began, I had no power
And now I have no will.

Hold

What do I expect
For what do I wait
What is it that I fear
will not last if late?
You are half-scared, surprised
What made me desperate?

I cannot explain
I am not even sure I know
A sense of incompleteness
That simply refuses to go
And knowing that if time runs out
The gaps will clearly show.

You wonder if this is madness
And sure, I wonder too,
When this urgency seizes me
As I sit and talk to you
Hoping it doesn't drive you away
And break my mind and heart in two.

Stay distant for a while, unhurt
Maybe this too shall pass by
And we will find time has
Proved the desperation a lie
And all that I sensed and felt was
The unwillingness to let die.

The Risk

Maybe it's not
That I am picky
You are just too
Forgetful perhaps
Maybe I thought
There was no need
To make promises
Rather than make
And then
Break them
Maybe you were
Trying so hard
To deny all feelings
That you didn't see
What were.

They might have grown,
They might have
Killed all I felt,
Perhaps;
You were so sure
This wasn't it
That you forgot to
open your mind
like you always taught me
you cared too much
for outside things
you backed out
without taking a step in.

Yes, life is all about
Meeting and moving
New people, new places
A constant adventure
Maybe we can
Save ourselves
Or maybe we can
Savour the risk
Who knows –
Depending on much
we are already hurt.
Think about it someday
When you are
Walking home
Because you were
Too sacred
To take the bus.

The Affair

The warmth of a summer morning
The chill of the winter night
You are the seasons
You are the reasons
For the spring and the flowers that delight.

A love so beautiful
A love with so much pain
You are the theme
You are the stream
That never flows back again.

A cold-hearted memory
A breath buried deep
You are the cry
You are the lie
That recklessness doth reap.

Inconstancy

You slam doors
into my face
and ask
the same old question
"What do you want?"
When I reply
you say,
"That's not the right answer
say it like this".
I repeat after you
puzzled, confused.

You open the door
and I'm met with
a new décor
I look at
the changed interior
while you caustically explain,
"I like it this way now".
I nod, and try
to like it too.

Each time I get back
It is the same story
The door slams
the answer changes
The inside is strange
unfriendly and cold
I try to like it again
Going around in circles.

It's like being on
the cloud, at the top
of the Faraway Tree
every week
a new land,
new people
new rules
At first, I felt
like you were rejecting me
each time the door slammed
Now I wonder
if the new décor meant
that you were rejecting you

I can think of
nothing to say to you
Even each night
as you haunt me
in my dreams
I can only watch and wait
the words silent
my eyes hostile and unsure
what did you want me to do?

There is no script
for me to follow
No instructions, no new answer
Everything I know is wrong
Now when you ask a question
I do not speak
You are surprised
wondering if I'd gone away
I dare not look
upon your face
lest it compels me to stay
My footsteps turn
as my heart
murmurs Adios
maybe some other day.

Fury of Love

I thought it was a love for all seasons,
But it was a love for no rhyme or reason
My love had a hate so blind
And a heart that was ruled by a mind
My love saw things that happened never
Congratulated itself for being smart and clever
My love believed only his assumption
And saw every act and word as pure treason
He hauled me to court, and called in the jury,
Set out on me with all his fury
He called me as a witness, to testify,
And all my protestations and justifications were called a lie.
He pounded on me with words to convince all
Laying out evidence, while I took the fall
I watched amazed, learning what I knew not,
And found myself nodding at this work of art.
'tis true I had lied, I cheated and I deceived,
Or how could the argument have been conceived?
So logical, so sure, definite without doubt
He does not lie, so how came it about?
I was guilty that I was free
I was guilty for choosing to be me
I was guilty for being kind
I was guilty of using my mind
I was guilty that I had cared for friends
I was guilty for trying to make amends
I was guilty that I had a past,
And because I was honest from the start,

My love was ruined because of me
And I had to pay to my heart's bankruptcy
I stepped down from the witness stand
There was nothing to say in my defence
My love looked lovely, proud he won
Certain at heart that justice was done
So what – it is only love we sacrificed
We will find others, it's the way of life
My love loved me for a season
That's that – no rhyme, no reason.

Idle Worship

I realize
I was a
minor necessity
at one point
in your goal
and now I'm not.
You talk of god
and a common love
en masse
You said you wanted
to bring me
closer to your god
I wonder if
you know
how much further
you pushed him
away from me

Your god
it appears to me
wants human sacrifice,
a homage of
tears, pain, suffering
he revels in it – a pagan god.
He talks of
connecting
without attachments
of love
without sensitivity,
he talks of
becoming god
without being even human
he talks of
'belonging' to him – a selfish god.

He talks to you
sends you signs
that direct your path
visions which
you must follow
a few magic words
that shares
his power with you
and a palm
poised to say 'Stop'.

He tells you
his children
are tainted and impure
they live in filth
and must be cleansed.
He tells you
when their uses
are through,
they can be
exiled.
He holds you tight
but orders you
to let go;
he demands to relate to you
and insists you let
your relationships die.
He kills your heart
and says 'Love'.

He is your god
never mine.
He that says
"Respect not
care not,
preserve your purity
for it belongs to me,
knowledge is power
use it selectively,
he is mine
that who comes first!"
In my godless world
My step is light
My heart is free.

Distances

You were my friend once
There were no reasons
We were – that's all we knew
Never sought beyond two
It was simple, quite simple really
I had you to complete me
It was enough; no questions there
All that mattered was that we cared.
When you left, it felt alright
We could never be out of sight
We were as one in our hearts
No distance could ever tear us apart.

Today we seek to answer why
We redefine what's You and I
We have to state how
We can be friends now
So far away, so far apart
Can we retain former love?
Can we ourselves alone
Weather all the storms?
A shoulder, a smile,
Cannot travel miles
And as we seek solace
In a different face
Can we return and find anew
The love that we once knew?

The Last Tribute

He wanted
A marriage
Kids and family
And guarantees.

He condemned
That I cared
That I shared
He wanted it completely.

He resented
My honesty
My loyalties
He could not trust me.

I asked for understanding
For the promises
For the love
A conspiracy.

He hit back
Hurting me
Abusing me
I made him angry.

He would not be moved
No change of mind
He would not tolerate
Being second priority.

I checked in vain
For other names
In my diaries
and my poetry.

I pleaded innocence
Explaining
Begging
Losing my sanity.

He twisted words
To suit his belief
A web of lies
That only he could see

How does
Imagination
Get to be more powerful
Than reality?

I stumbled and fell
He waited till
Someone held me
And called it infidelity.

He turned around
Threw a derisive glance
Walked away
Self-righteously.

He won
I lost
Proven
Guilty.

I was shot for betrayal
No trial
No lawyers
No jury.

A lonely funeral
After all, who wants
to watch a dead horse
flogged needlessly?

I wondered at so
Elaborate a plan
Only because
He loved me?

Unclaimed

Why did you call me back
When you were not there?
I had left to go home
having realized life is seldom fair

My mind had reconciled
that you had places to go
Is it that you always want
to see me wait at your door?

I pace about missing you
unable to move on, unable to stay
I wonder if you know what it means
for a heart to lie on the driveway?

I look at the same sky you see
The same moon and stars every night
I turn restless in my sleep
Why is your face always in sight?

When will you return or will you?
What if I waiting, die?
Will you blame me for my impatience,
or rue my weakness and sigh?

By the time we meet
My face will be unknown to you
We may have to begin afresh,
But will the heart still be true?

My heart cannot be on hold
Till you deliberate
Adios, this is not to be, for
as long as I could, I did wait.

You seem to be taking your time
and I can wait no longer
Read the note I left for you saying
I wish I had been stronger.

I Stopped Dreaming

I stopped dreaming
A few nights ago
Was it
The night that you left
Or the night when I woke
Maybe
We'll never know
Because I stopped dreaming
A long time ago.

It was Autumn I think
When the leaves were just beginning to fall from trees
Or was it the Rain
When waves lashed mercilessly in the sea
Maybe it was Summer
When meadows were filled with the hum of bees
Or faithful old Winter
Gently whitening our lives in unseen degrees.

It was a time like any other
That's why I don't remember
I don't know.
Yet, its touch
Lingers on in my soul.
I had dreamed my last dream
Seen you the last time
Ages and ages ago
Yet when?
I do not know.

Care to Value

It's so wonderful to know
your friends are always there
Those who will always stand by you
through the dark side and the fair

Friends see your worst failings
Making it so easy
To deplore your petty ways,
your meanness and your jealousies

Yet they hold your hand
and with you they'll be
In spite of vile moods and tempers
in spite of unfairness and insecurities.

You can tell them your darkest secret
share your weakest fears
They match smile for a smile
a tear for every tear.

Accursed are those who see not
and abuse the gift of their care
and weep to have lost them
only when Death makes them aware.

The Wait – I

When you know
It might be too late
Distances widen
And time will not wait
Shall we then
Look around us and say,
"Why did you not
Tell me that day?"
We did not hear
The silence call
We let things
Build a wall
Someday, perchance
When we meet again
How shall we adjudge
The losses and the gains?

Unbegun

We'll never be through
Because we will never begin
An incident that never happened
A story never told
When Truth will stand up
And proclaim its Innocence
It will see,
Tears that were never shed
Smiles that never reached the eyes.

Death

I woke up one morning
To find all the colours gone
There were no birds but crows
There were no flowers, only stones.

There is something awful
About the colour white
It is like a quiet stillness
As dark as the dead of night

Time is but a set of numbers
To the body which under the sheet lay
The sky had turned brighter though
As if you had passed that way.

Silences and Words

She came often and sat by me
I would have said intrusively
And even though I moved away
She chatted to me every day.

I usually never said a word
Hoping she might be deterred
Yet she always stayed on track
While I simply held back.

We met 16 years day by day
How could there be more to say?
She let me get on with my things
Always waiting by the wings.

And then suddenly I found
She seemed not to be around
Now that just seemed very strange
For I was within hearing range.

I searched for her high and low
Wondering where she could go
The silence was getting uneasy
Had she given up on me?

Hoping to mollify I started to speak
From years to days, months to weeks
Every word that I knew
In thought and speech and writing too.

Why had I not shared
When she was sitting there?
Now she's passed, silenced for ever
Whatever I say now cannot matter.

Voids

I was surprised
At being alive
After you were gone
For I, deprived,
Of a love so deep
Could never survive
I was certain
I would die.

I kept living
And rued my fate
For love seemed weaker
Than I could state
Mortal fallacies –
An emotional rebate
I doubted love
At any rate.

Yet, when I walked
Alone in the street,
I would hope
To no one meet
My eyes turned down
To my feet
My lips had no
Words to greet.

I watched the stars
Come out at night
And the moon
shine its light
Sunrise, dewdrops, rainbows,
Dawn, dusk, twilight,
There was no change
For human sight.

Watching myself
From somewhere without,
Each street, song, chore,
Stirs the emptiness about
Conscious of loneliness
Uncertainty and doubt
A void tears my body
throughout.

I try to feel myself
Through a hard crust
Of an empty shell
Crumbling to dust
I will continue
As I must
Knowing that life
Is rarely just.

Solitude

I need no one
to listen now
no one to care
for when I speak somehow
there's no one there.

My voice comes back
bouncing off deaf walls
and though they nod sagely,
they lack the depth to hear its call.

I need no one's hand to hold
no shoulder to cry
For when the night gets cold,
the fires die.

The chill returns to me
seeking warmth at my side
Blind men don't come out to see
a firework's night.

I need no friend, no presence
I just need to be alone
for mine is where I am
carrying what I own.

I need space around me
And time to shift things about
I need no distrustful emotions to be
I can be within without.

An Inward Journey

I wish I could
Shut myself away
From the world
For just one day
    And be with myself.

With the constraints
Of daily routine
And the pressures
Of work piling in
    I've been so busy.

That I've had no time
to share confidences
The space only
Strengthened defences
    We had to repair bridges.

We needed to talk
and ask of the other
If she was comfortable
Or did she suffer
    while one made choices.

To find out if
we still agreed
Or was the will
of one buried
    for lack of consultation.

How far had we come
From what we were
The differences that bred
The thoughts that differed
    While each hurried on.

We were yet one
And would always be
For without the other,
We would be incomplete
    Then who'd cross the wall?

The distance had to be
Just so much
For beyond that
We'd be out of touch
    With no hope of return.

Touch Me Not

You put the fear
Of people into me
If you couldn't
Accept my warmth,
Why did you
Give me your chill?
I now freeze
When reaching out
And people wonder
What it's all about
I live closed
Inside of me
A prisoner
of my own fear
too proud to admit
too scared to leave
an iceberg adrift
in the People's sea.

Fear Not

Fear not
if you cannot see
in these words
a piece of me.

Perhaps, it is so,
perhaps so it must be;
In our dear love's waste
Is our constancy.

Crash

Be kind to me no more
Nothing is as it was before
I should have known in reality
We were never meant to be
I held on to the promises
Always believing
And then you step away
Saying you will be leaving
I hold my ravaged heart
Blurred words on a page
From all that you said
How could I this gauge?

Once again, as before,
a man jumps off the cliff
Never knowing if death was life
Or death is this.
Forever fated to love and to lose
Never realizing he had nothing to choose
It was foretold, it was pre-determined
But what sees a man who is blind?
Naive in his rapture, drunk in his despair,
He found you can borrow but never have
And as he crashes on rocks below
He learns at last to let go.

Regrets

And all the people I loved
And who now are dead
Their memories like mist
Swirl in my head.
And only the day I lie buried,
These thoughts will rest in me.

Till then reflected in every story
Will be the same plot
I will live again those final days
Every day in every thought
A ghost sitting in my mind
Poking every memory it finds.

The words I should have spoken
The hand I should have held
The time I should have taken
To show how much I cared.
Have no fear, I cannot forget
So sharp is the sting of regret.

Whatever Is, Is

No matter how hard you try
No matter how much you cry
No matter how deeply you miss,
Whatever is, is.

You could pray at every shrine
Wish on every star that shines
No matter what you promise,
Whatever is, is.

All your goodness rolled in one
Every favour you return
No matter what – that or this,
Whatever is, is.

It doesn't matter
It doesn't matter
No matter what
Whatever is, is.

Backing Off

I am sorry I forgot
That I don't know you well
And things I assume of you
Are things I cannot tell.

You are another person
A result of different experiences
Only you can know fake from true
And step beyond pretences.

To give your thoughts a label
To give your fears a name
I pre-suppose and conceive
That you and I are the same.

I am sorry I forgot
You are not me, can never be
You must remind me time and again
I am not the centre of gravity.

Trust

In the middle of life
I was suddenly told
It's a myth that
We are friends of old

We stopped being friends
A long time ago
How could it be
That I did not know?

You had long gone
As had the years in me
I know now that nothing
Is ever what it seems to be.

Remainder

I have lived 17 days
And failed to understand why
You are gone
And with you so have I.

I have been with people
I ate, worked, read and slept
Life seems to insist on returning
And I have no way to keep her back.

It's as though nothing happened
The only trace is in my heart
Is it real or just a dream
That you and I did part?

I talk about you and things we did
To anybody who will hear
And, to my dismay, will go on
For another four score years

When will I end,
Or when will this pain?
How long can I carry within me
My mortal remains?

Endurance

Do you know how hard it is
to stay strong
when your insides are corroding
all day long?

It chips away at you
causing slivers of pain
And every tiny memory
can make you feel it again

It's a boulder kept
at the centre of your chest
That wakes you up at 4 am
and lets you have no rest.

To hold the burning tears
in your eyes lest they fall
To bite back anger and apologies
to stay stiff and stand tall.

Some people are made of sterner stuff,
but to say that of me would be a lie
for there is just so much I can take
before I simply lay down and die.

Mirrors

In a room full of mirrors,
There are only reflections
They laugh together
Weep together
True always to each other
Yet none can reach out
trapped in their frame
when you move,
they all follow
limited, helpless
unable to make
any change.

It was my life
That writhed
while they
stood and watched
Suffering with me
from a safe distance
Like my pain
was infectious
afraid of being hurt
by the flailing.
It was my reflection
and it didn't
touch me.

The Outsider

Time and again I was reminded
that I really had no rights
I must stand outside the door
till I am beckoned inside

There was a place for me to wait
Just so many words to use
And no matter how humbly I begged
it was so easy to refuse

Friends could come and go at ease
Strangers were welcome too
But once you are an outsider,
There is nothing you can do

Cruelty comes in many forms
The wounds don't have to show
How much more dead are the living,
no one can ever really know.

Choices

I found myself
while you were away
You thought you'd find me here,
but I did not stay

So much changes
with the passage of time
Love looks different now
than it did in its prime

When we met again
so much was new
I was not me
and you were not you

We looked at each other
with new eyes
searching for the familiar
a faint memory of our lives

There was nothing
we could hold
no words to sieve
no habits of old

Was it worth it
to begin again
to seek a love we loved
to wade through all the pain?

It seemed too much of a risk
we had no strength to fail
We had once loved and lost
and sworn off the trail.

What could have been,
we can never know
I fear too much to guide this road
Whatever must will be so.

This is what we
made of us
Wound up in tears
and deep distrust.

It is as it was
meant to be
You are this you
and I am this me

There is no turning back
all regrets are in vain
If we returned to where we were,
We would still be here yet again.

Flight into Freedom...

I have almost never thought
Of what is right and what is not
As society says so it is
Never pausing or wanting to contradict.
To realize I am free
I needed my individuality
Buried in my social fears
Its voice I just could not hear
Deaf was I, also blind
For I did not even see the mind
Handicapped thus I was so
Crippled for I could never go
Out of me to reach to you
A wall I couldn't break through
Content was I, or thought I was
Never feeling closed in because
I knew not what freedom meant
Or that it was alright to be different
I had choices I could make at will
And people would respect me still.

Yet, the clouds did clear one day
When towards me you made your way
Took my hand and led me out
Told me what it was all about
That I needn't stay in prison
That everything grew under the sun
I was unsure, but I tried
And much to my mind's delight

I found myself, thanks to you
My choices, my freedom,
came flooding through.
Life came alive to me
I almost had new eyes to see
I saw beauty in every place
The natural intelligence of time and space
Books became much more than words
Society became just a people's herd

And then slowly and surely it began
I'm not sure exactly when
Your grip tightened, your fingers hurt
My freedom was a bruised bird
Pressure of demands weighed on me
I was enchained by loyalty
I tried to tell you so much how
Obligations were meaningless now
Your friendship was precious to me
But not more than liberty
Accept me, why not, as I am,
Rather than have me pretend
Wouldn't it be much more true
If in my freedom I chose you?
Try to understand what I say
For it was you who showed me the way
Maybe I will stumble further
But we are not responsible for each other.

My friend, if at a fork we part
The schism is not in our hearts.
I carry your light within my soul
To guide me when I get cold
Our fingers are forever entwined
As your heart blends with mine.
You may stand across from me
But we have a solidarity
We are individuals, we will differ
Our sum total may be a cipher
But relate we can and always will
Warm each other in the chill
When the dawn comes, we will rise
To meet again another time.

Power

There were conditions
Described in great depth
Instructions to follow
Laid down at every step

Every rule must be learnt
Every word used consciously
Even a single foible
Will cost you very dearly.

They squeeze till you cry
And beat till you break
And when you fail their tests
They burn you at the stake

Those that such power possess,
Must feel so very great
To grab a fistful of righteousness
And turn love into hate.

Expectations

It seemed a sham
to not be who I am
But you said you'd like me more
if I was different from
who I was before.

No matter the hues I took
and the many shades,
You found it wanting every time
a flaw at every stage

I feared I would lose you
and it happened all the same
You said I kept changing
and you couldn't trust me again

I had been so many versions
I was losing track
I only knew that someday I had
to find myself back

I still lost you anyway
and oh! The irony
'twas cause I ceased to be
the person that was me.

Stone Walled

Your heart hardened
turning to stone
You pushed away everyone
so you could be alone

It's not the deepest love
That cannot forgive
It is the arrogance of ego
That won't let you live

You lose people you love
only because of pride
You hold on to you and yours
and fasten windows on all sides

Now safe in your prison,
You can neither give nor take
and in this righteous illusion
A contentment you fake

The time we have been given
will never come again
We can die bitter and stupid
smug in our self-restrain

How does something so foolish deserve breath
that has no respect for life and none for death?
Who other than humans could be so insane
and look, it's raining porcupines again!

The Wait – II

You said you were tired
and that I was late
distances had widened
and time did not wait.

I had been walking on the path
that would lead me to you
and though I knew you were waiting,
There was so much to do.

I believed you would wait
right till the end
You had promised me
you'd always be my friend.

In every step I walked,
you were always in my sight
no matter how weary I felt,
you were my beacon of light

You thought that I had
lost my way
that I did not mean to
meet you that day

From where you were waiting,
you could not see me
So while I moved towards you,
you moved away from me

And every stone on the way
and every tree my witness be
wheresoever my heart did rove
it always belonged to thee

The Murder

Have you ever taken a life
Stabbed into someone a serrated knife?
Have you ever tried to kill?
Squeeze till a body went still?

It all begins in the end
Never thought it would be a friend
It's a story that's never old
Forever in books and poems retold.

Denial in the very first stage
Turning slowly into rage
All the questions, all the fears
The disbelief and the tears

Love finds hurt in many places
Mostly in loved familiar faces
And even though you never knew it,
It was only love that 'made me do it'

It's happened before, it will happen again
Love feels hurt and love causes pain
And as the knife twists further inside,
You know now that it was all a lie

Love Destroys

To love is a lie
The blinding emotion
of forever
is just a name
for uncontrolled insanity
which wears away with time
in who's so-called
rich tapestry
space digs holes.
A feeling who's pleasure
is so great
that it drives you senseless
But whose torment
is merciless,
random and unrelenting
And yet,
it reigns not
except in madness
It can destroy the very soul
just like hate
What then is love?
A dangerous lunatic's
intense passion
to die or let die?
It is the stuff
people say that
music and poetry
is made of

The beauty of which
lies incomparable
Yet each of which
is far more controlled,
calls for sense and reason.
Beyond its
natural boundaries
lies a cacophony
deafening,
harsh,
repetitive,
senseless
Love breaks people,
destroys minds.

The Life Sentence

Where can you go
to build your life anew
When all you have is broken
and there's nothing you can do
No matter how much you change,
Your past will always be there

People will always remind you
of your fallacies and flaws
For their fears, their pain and misery
you will always be the cause
And you can never be the person you could be
because of what once was

You wake up every morning
your mind freshly set
Resolved to be different
to do nothing to regret
But people find it hard to forgive
and harder to forget

Is there anywhere to go
Where I can be me
People who understand
And have fresh eyes to see
That no one is perfect
we can only try to be

Once the sentence is passed,
There is no recourse
Nothing can redeem you
Neither will nor any force
You are hereby sentenced
To a life-time of remorse.

Hurt

You hurt.
It's not even pain
just a slow erosion
like skin peeling
from the inside
a hungry ulcer
the subtle darkening
of the lungs

Your hurt
It has made home
inside of me
Every single day,
I feel it grow
it plays with my mind
and pokes holes
in my soul

The hurt
sears like a mad fire
Coursing through me
cruel and relentless
waking me all night
bleeding through my eyes
and you don't
know anything

Stone Hearts

For the thoughts that haunt me
I cannot close my eyes
for every moment, every footstep
vain hope rises and quickly dies

If life were made of chances
And dreams were meant to live,
I would hear your voice call my name
Saying forget and forgive.

But there are no real choices
and dreams are only dust
Favour from a benevolent god
praying it would be just

for the pain that tears me,
I cannot close my eyes
The stone that is now my heart,
Strangely only cries

Control

From the very beginning
You called the shots
What I could do
and what I could not

You made me wash my hands
You had me tie up my hair
So much I could understand
for you had a baby to care

The silences were growing
and tension filled the air
When I stood at the door,
Not a glance would you spare

Unheedful I still returned
the baby and I had bonded so well
And you my friend of many years,
retreated into a shell

Anything I said or did
seemed to cause offense
I accepted every accusation
and apologized in defence

With others you were always fine
Everything they did was right
With them you talked and walked and shopped
and isolated me from your life

You curtailed my time
more and more
It was like you were
settling a score

I begged and pleaded
you said you did not care
Your dismissal of my hurt
was more than I could bear.

You were a friend
that I had held so dear
It seemed only I felt that way
because now your message was clear

I was an outsider
to you and your family
and that's why it mattered not
the pain you brought to me

It took me a long time
to get your intent
I was no longer welcome
and that is what you meant

My love for the baby
will linger in my heart still
But stay away from you
I can and I will.

You pushed me out
and shut the door
I was welcome to
your house no more

How could you not
feel my pain
and do that to me
over and over again?

You said I was
the one to blame
That things would never
be the same

All that you told me
was that everything was wrong
and that in your life,
I did not belong.

I walked away
my heart was broken
filled with words
that were never spoken

Had you just let me know
I had to stay in my place,
You'd never have had to shut
the door in my face.

You can be who you are
and accept that, I must
but look out your door and you
will find
shattered pieces of my trust.

The House of Cards

It was a house of cards
and it came tumbling down
We knew it was fragile
and we carefully tiptoed around

It was all we had
held together by a thread
And in spite of everything that went wrong,
we hoped that time would make it strong

The touch was meant to steady
maybe the force was too much
It had held out for as long as it could
the weather has gotten too rough

Cracks had widened beyond repair
Cards were scattered everywhere
Maybe the missing ones had weakened it
or the broken ones that did not fit

What way could one judge the loss
how could one measure the pain
All that our hearts could resolve
was never to build a house of cards again.

Wasted Love

When I started to walk,
I had known where I wanted to go
so sure I was of my tread,
I cared not for friend or foe

Somewhere along the way,
you called out my name
It would cause some delay
but nonetheless I came

You were desolate and wanted to talk
I from my journey was weary
It felt nice to share kind words
You got your coffee, I had my tea

We looked at different directions,
but wished to walk together
We had promised to be friends
in sunshine and rainy weather

How could we walk on the other's path
when we had different journeys to make
confused, without purpose or direction,
there were decisions to take

We called it betrayal
the comfort too hard to leave
that we were headed to different lands
our hearts refused to believe

We turned upon each other
Such is human frailty
Ensuring we felt no sense of choice
Just made parting so easy

And the God that sat in heaven
sighed in deep disappointment
as once again two hearts
wasted all the love he had sent.

Flowers of May – II

She was the sunshine of Spring
And the flowers of May
The path where the tall trees beckoned
Where I hoped to return some day.

And as one path led on to another
I wandered back so late
A stone marked the place she sat
To tell me she could no longer wait.

A birdsong conveyed
The message she had left
Of a trust that lay broken
A promise I never kept.

The seat in the meadows
Lies vacant and empty
The flowers of May that beckoned
Had vanished along with thee.

Acknowledgements

Every poem in this compilation is a result of my experiences with people in my life. They taught me valuable lessons and forced an insight on me that found expression in these words. The family is always the first school, and no matter the circumstances, I can only feel gratitude to my parents Anil and Leela Saraf who developed in me a fondness for books and an appreciation of poetry early in life.

My sisters Alpana, Archana and Vivechana were my scaffolding through my younger years, and growing up with them brought to me the richness of diversity in personalities and both, the strength of an ego and the softness of humility. Special thanks to my English teacher Mrs. Manju Mehra who nurtured the instinct in me to write, and my friend Meeta who left us too soon and introduced me to the deepest forms of love and pain.

Lastly my heartfelt gratitude to those who pushed, supported and encouraged me to publish my poetry. I acknowledge the brilliant imagery and sensitivity of Soulscapes, my publisher, who designed and illustrated the sensibilities with care and insight; my friends Shyama and Meenakshi who typed, proofed and critiqued my poems to let the best shine; and of course, Gayatri Mazumdar of Brown Critique for her amazing editing and guidance.

Thank you!

www.ingramcontent.com/pod-product-compliance
Lightning Source LLC
LaVergne TN
LVHW041735190726
843493LV00008B/2352